MY FIRST LOOK AT HOLIDAYS

EASTER IS A SPRING HOLIDAY

Easter

AARON FRISCH

CREATIVE EDUCATION

Published by Creative Education

123 South Broad Street, Mankato, Minnesota 56001

Creative Education is an imprint of The Creative Company

Designed by Rita Marshall

Photographs by Archive Photos, Sonia Halliday, Donald Kelly, Terrance Klassen, Mrs.

Kevin Scheibel, Unicorn Stock Photos (Gary Johnson, Martha McBride), The Viesti

Collection (Trip)

Cover illustration © 1996 Roberto Innocenti

Printed in the United States of America

Library of Congress Cataloging-in-Publication Data

Frisch, Aaron. Easter / by Aaron Frisch.

p. cm. — (My first look at holidays)

ISBN 1-58341-367-7

I. Easter—Juvenile literature. I. Title.

GT4935.F75 2005   394.2667—dc22   2004057097

First edition 9 8 7 6 5 4 3 2 1

EASTER

THE EASTER STORY

Easter is a **holiday** for people called "Christians." Christians believe that a man named Jesus was God's son. Jesus lived a long time ago.

Some people did not like the things Jesus said about God. So they killed him. They nailed him to a **cross**. Christians believe Jesus came back to life three days later on Easter.

A CHURCH WINDOW SHOWING AN EASTER SCENE

The days before Easter are a sad time for Christians. They remember how Jesus died. But Easter Sunday is a happy day. Many Christians go to church on Easter morning. They listen to Bible stories and remember how Jesus came back to life.

Christians believe that

when they die,

they will go to **Heaven**

and see Jesus.

MANY PEOPLE GO TO CHURCH ON EASTER

Bright and New

Easter is not on the same day every year. But it is always on a Sunday in spring. Spring is a time when plants start to grow and baby animals are born. Many people think of Easter as a holiday of new life.

You see rabbits in many Easter decorations. This might be because rabbits have lots of babies in the spring. Many decorations also show white lambs or yellow **chicks**.

People used to buy

new clothes for Easter.

Some people still do.

Many Easter clothes are white.

FANCY EASTER HATS CALLED BONNETS

White is the color of Easter. This is because it looks bright and new. Flowers are popular decorations on Easter. Many people decorate churches and homes with big, white flowers called Easter lilies.

Holiday Foods

Many families eat a special dinner on Easter. Ham and turkey are popular Easter foods. In some parts of the world, people eat special buns, too. They are called "hot cross buns" because they have a frosting cross on top.

THIS FLOWER IS CALLED AN EASTER LILY

Some people make Easter eggs. They boil eggs in water. Then they decorate the shells with colorful **dyes**. Some people use crayons or stickers, too. The eggs can then be eaten or set out as decorations.

The 40 days before Easter
are called Lent.
Many Christians do not
eat meat on Fridays during Lent.

The Easter Bunny

Some kids believe in the Easter Bunny. The Easter Bunny is a big rabbit that visits houses on Easter. He hides baskets of candy for people to find.

THE EASTER BUNNY LEAVES BASKETS OF TREATS

On Easter morning, grown-ups or the Easter Bunny may hide eggs. Kids then "hunt" for the Easter eggs. Some kids play games with the eggs. They roll them down a hill to see which one cracks last!

Eggs, colorful candy, and games are all part of the fun of Easter. It is a time for people to be happy as they remember Jesus and welcome spring!

CHOCOLATE EGGS ARE A POPULAR EASTER CANDY

HANDS-ON: MAKING EASTER EGGS

Easter eggs are fun to make anytime!

WHAT YOU NEED

Hard-boiled eggs (with white shells)
Crayons

WHAT YOU DO

Have a contest with your friends or family. See who can make the best Easter egg! Draw a bunny face. Write your name or "Happy Easter" in big letters. Cover the egg with lots of colorful swirls. Draw a little Easter picture on one side. Or cover the egg in polka dots. When you are done, you can show off your egg . . . and then eat it!

People have been making
Easter eggs for hundreds of
years. Some people today
fill plastic eggs with candy.

EASTER EGGS CAN BE DECORATED IN MANY WAYS

Index

Words to Know

chicks—the babies of chickens or other birds

cross—two big pieces of wood that are shaped like a "t"

dyes—liquids that are used to color things

Heaven—the place where God lives

holiday—a special day that happens every year

Read More

Chambers, Catherine. *Easter*. Austin, Tex.: Steck-Vaughn, 1999.

Merrick, Patrick. *Easter Bunnies*. Chanhassen, Minn.: Child's World, 1999.

Wildsmith, Brian. *The Easter Story*. Grand Rapids, Mich.: Eerdman's Books, 2000.

Explore the Web

Easter and Spring Crafts http://www.enchantedlearning.com/crafts/easter

Easter for Kids http://www.rexanne.com/easter-kids.html

Easter for Kids and Teachers http://www.kiddyhouse.com/Holidays/Easter